AS GOOD AS
GOLDA

AS GOOD AS GOLDA

The warmth and wisdom of

Israel's Prime Minister

COMPILED AND EDITED BY

Israel and Mary Shenker

THE McCALL PUBLISHING COMPANY
New York

Library of Congress Catalog Card Number: 74-114843

SBN 8415-0029-0

The McCall Publishing Company

230 Park Avenue, New York, N.Y. 10017

Printed in the United States of America

Contents

foreword

Golda Meir is a woman of many parts: wit, strength of purpose, unabashed sentiment, and an ability to reduce complicated issues to manageable dimensions.

Every one of these qualities is precious, for no other leader has her problems: a permanent state of war with half a dozen foreign enemies, frequent incomprehension abroad, as many kibitzers at home as there are citizens, and the need to keep Israel a land of immigration—which means ever more kibitzers ready to give more advice.

Mrs. Meir has spent much of her own life as a kibitzer (she cooked up policies in her Tel Aviv kitchen even when she was out of government), and also as an immigrant.

Golda (she is best known by her first name) was born May 3, 1898, in Kiev, Russia. Her parents were impoverished, and in 1906 the family emigrated to the United States, where they were hardly better off. Golda's father worked as a carpenter, and her mother ran a small grocery.

Golda's first conflict was one of generations. At fourteen she ran away from her parents' home in Milwaukee, and went to live with an older sister in Denver. There she met her future husband, Morris Myerson, another émigré from Russia. Returning home when she was eighteen, Golda plunged into a confusion of enthusiasms: Zionism, Socialism, teaching, public speaking. She even persuaded the reluctant

Myerson to go to Palestine—and married him once he agreed. The two left for the Holy Land in 1921.

The Myersons settled in a kibbutz, and Golda said afterward that she was accepted only because she had brought along a phonograph and records. Her job was taking care of the chickens, but her interests were broader and she was chosen kibbutz representative to the Histadrut—the General Federation of Labor.

When her husband could bear communal life no longer, the Myersons moved to Tel Aviv, and later to Jerusalem. They were living there when Golda gave birth to a son, Menachem, and a daughter, Sara. Some years later Golda took in the laundry in Menachem's boarding school to pay for his tuition, and her husband worked as a carpenter. It was a grim time for both parents. (Myerson died in 1951. Today Menachem is a cellist in the United States; Sara lives in a kibbutz.)

During World War II, Golda was a member of the War Economic Advisory Council set up by the British, who then controlled Palestine. When the war ended, she worked for the clandestine entry into Palestine of Jewish immigrants, and sponsored a hunger strike in sympathy with them.

When leaders of the Zionist movement were arrested by the British in 1946, Golda was one of the few left free. The Jews in Palestine thereupon got their first experience of Golda's running things, as she took over Zionist negotiations with the British. At the same time, she kept in close touch with leaders of the Jewish armed resistance—who opposed the British and also fought against Arab terrorists.

Since a war of independence seemed imminent, she left for America to raise money for weapons, despite warnings that she should not expect much help there. In less than three months she collected $50 million.

Returning home, Golda undertook delicate political negotiations. She traveled to Amman (now capital of Jordan) disguised as an Arab woman, to urge King Abdullah to keep his promise not to join other Arab leaders in an attack on the Jews. Her hazardous mission ended in failure when

Abdullah went back on his promise. In 1948, after joining her colleagues in signing Israel's independence declaration, Golda (bearing the first Israeli passport) went to the United States to raise money for her new country's vital needs. Her government then named her Israel's first Ambassador to the Soviet Union. Despite the oppression of the Soviet regime, Jews of the city flocked to Moscow's central synagogue to welcome her and express their solidarity with the State of Israel.

Golda entered the Israeli Cabinet in 1949, having finally managed to make the Moscow embassy run as a kibbutz—with everyone, including the Ambassador, taking turns at the chores. Seven years later she became Foreign Minister, and presided over the policy of establishing friendships with the new nations of Asia and Africa.

The Premier was David Ben-Gurion, and he had a great influence on Golda. A man of strong ideas and enormous will, he even prevailed on strong-willed Golda to Hebraicize her name to Meir—which means "illuminates." But when Ben-Gurion split with Levi Eshkol (Israel's third Premier and Golda's predecessor in the office), Golda sided with Eshkol. Indeed, she was the strongest supporter Eshkol had; it was fashionable to say that hers was the stiffest backbone in the Cabinet.

After the 1965 elections, Golda resigned as Foreign Minister—and then became Secretary-General of Mapai, the Labor Party. On Eshkol's death, in March, 1969, the party selected her as its candidate for the Premier's job. When she presented her government to the Knesset (Parliament), she won the biggest vote of confidence in Israel's history.

Seven months later, Golda headed the Mapai ticket in national parliamentary elections—and the party again emerged as the country's largest vote getter. That put Golda, who can stand the heat, right back in the Number One kitchen of policy—the Premier's office.

What follows in this book is Golda's wisdom from that kitchen, as well as from her speeches, interviews, reports, and conversations over the course of many years.

such a woman

"There is a type of woman who cannot remain at home. In spite of the place her children and family fill in her life, her nature demands something more; she cannot divorce herself from the larger social life. She cannot let her children narrow her horizon. For such a woman, there is no rest."

"If only political leaders would allow themselves to feel, as well as to think, the world might be a happier place."

Golda was once guest of honor at an editors' lunch in New York. When the chicken came wrapped in ham, the waiter said to her in Hebrew, "If you don't want to eat this, I'll give you something else."

"How come you speak Hebrew?" she asked, and he explained that he came from Israel.

"What did you do in Israel?" Golda demanded.

"I was a waiter."

"So for this you had to come to America?"

In a discussion on deferred payments, Golda said: "You can't fry fish in July with oil you get in September."

"A strong people does not have to demonstrate the justice of its demands. A weak people, even when it has demonstrated the justice of its demands, has still not done enough."

Just before the 1967 war, Premier Levi Eshkol delivered a radio address to his nation, and was criticized because he stumbled over his words. Golda said afterward: "A leader who doesn't hesitate before he sends his nation into battle is not fit to be a leader."

Commenting on a rivalry between two Israeli leaders, Golda said: "I would like to see the war with the Arabs finished before 'the war of the Jews' * begins."

"Anybody who believes in something without reservation, believes that this thing is right and should be, has the stamina to meet obstacles and overcome them. The best example, of course, is somebody who is very, very religious, who honestly and sincerely believes. He has an enormous source of strength. From my early youth I believed in two things: one, the need for Jewish sovereignty, so that Jews—and this has become a cliché—can be master of their own fate; and two, a society based on justice and equality, without exploitation. But I was never so naive or foolish as to think that if you merely believe in something it happens. You must struggle for it."

Reminded of the great emotional response of Soviet Jewry to her arrival in Moscow in 1948, Golda rejoined: "If you had sent a broomstick to Moscow, and said it represented the State of Israel, it would have received the same welcome."

* *The War of the Jews* is the title of a book by the first-century historian Josephus.

"The tragedy of our generation is that, after the two World Wars, long drawn-out discussions on disarmament are held as though we had a choice between war and peace. Ever since Isaiah spoke of the day when swords would be beaten into plowshares, mankind has made revolutionary strides in all domains—but the sword is still in use and many fields are still untilled for lack of the plow."

"There should be some place on earth where there is a Jewish majority. As a minority we have quite a history."

"A woman who had worked zealously for the Zionist cause came to one of the Zionist offices and said: 'Is this what I get for all the work? My son wants to go and live in Israel.' "

On hearing that Mario Procaccino, candidate for mayor of New York City, was once a teacher, ex-teacher Golda said: "You gave that up for politics?"

"We need strength not only to stand fast along the borders, but also to keep quiet. We must develop the power of silence. I am not prepared to make declarations at a time when there is no occasion for them. We have too many people who talk too much."

When her Chief of Cabinet suggested something for her to say to waiting journalists, Golda rejoined: "You can't improve on saying nothing."

When the Israeli Cabinet was trying to deal with a series of assaults on women, one Minister suggested that women should not be allowed on the streets after dark. Golda protested: "Men are attacking the women, not the other way around. If there is going to be a curfew, let the men be locked up, not the women."

"In a society where each one lives for himself—today we live, tomorrow we will be gone—there is nothing. The greatest challenge to leaders and educators is to bring idealism into the picture despite the cloud that hangs over humanity."

"In Russia the authorities are trying to root out Judaism, so there is no danger of assimilation. In America, where you are free to be Jewish, the danger of assimilation is great."

"Zionism and pessimism are not compatible."

Golda is always telling people: "Don't be so humble—you're not that great."

"A teacher is one who has a program—arithmetic, reading, writing, and so on—fulfills it conscientiously, and feels that he has done his job. An educator tries to give children something else in addition: spirit."

the desert of hate

❀ ❀

"There is nothing Israel wants so much as peace. There is nothing Israel needs so much as peace. With all the bleakness of the desert, the desert of hate around us is even more bleak."

❀

"Many people have lost wars, and many people's countries have been occupied by foreign powers. Our history is much more tragic. Hitler took care of six million Jews. If we lose a war, that's the end forever—and we disappear from the earth. If one fails to understand this, then one fails to understand our obstinacy."

"We intend to remain alive. Our neighbors want to see us dead. This is not a question that leaves much room for compromise."

"No people in the world knows collective eulogies as well as the Jews do. But we have no intention of going down in order that some should speak well of us."

"It's a big mistake to think the reason for the conflict between us is territory. They don't want us here. That's what it's about. It isn't true that they don't want us in Nablus or Jenin. They don't want us, period."

"We refuse, absolutely, to be the one people in the world which consents to having its fate decided by others."

"We have our backs against the wall. We don't even have a wall. We have a sea. The only friendly neighbor we have is the Mediterranean."

"I oppose anyone who questions the morality of our being in the territories occupied as a result of the war launched against us for the purpose of extermination. It is the essence of morality to ensure the survival of the Jewish people in the Jewish state."

"Security represents an extreme burden for Israel, and if we have to do even more the burden will increase. Yet there is no limit to what we can take. How much pain can one bear before one dies? This nation won't die, won't commit suicide."

"Our secret weapon: No alternative."

"The Jewish people have held out for two thousand years, and as long as we, the children—and our children—are alive, Israel will be defended to the last drop of Jewish blood."

"Those who were killed in the gas chambers by Hitler were the last Jews to die without defending themselves."

"You cannot be a little bit alive and a little bit dead to accommodate your neighbors."

"Those who attack Israel should not be surprised if they are hit sevenfold in response."

"If we have to cut our standard of living, if we have to do with very little, we will do it. If the Arabs have the illusion that because they can't shoot us they will starve us, or that because we don't like to starve we'll raise a white flag and beg for mercy, they are doomed to disappointment."

"I understand the Arabs wanting to wipe us out, but do they really expect us to cooperate?"

"Do you think we're so particular whether we die by nuclear weapons or conventional weapons?"

"We are said to be intelligent and rational people, and are therefore expected to bury our dead quietly."

"A wonderful people these Israelis! They win wars every ten years, whatever the odds. And they have done it again. Fantastic! Now that they have won this round, let them go back where they came from, so that Syrian gunners on the Golan Heights can again shoot into the kibbutzim, so that Jordanian Legionnaires on the towers of the Old City can again shell at will, so that the Gaza Strip can again be a nest for terrorists, so that the Sinai Desert can again become the staging ground for Nasser's divisions."

"Attacks on the frontiers, sabotage attempts within Israel, and attacks of piracy against Israelis abroad have fortified our resolve never to return to the situation of constant peril which prevailed before the Six-Day War."

"We're told over and over again that Nasser is humiliated. Humiliated as a result of what? He wanted to destroy us, and—poor man—he failed. Somehow I just can't bring myself to feel too sorry for him."

"If there is anything that has horrified me in the past years, it is not that people criticize us. That is absolutely legitimate, even if we don't like it and we'd rather hear praise. What does horrify me is that murderers are played up as heroes, and that suddenly the Arabs are waging a 'war of liberation' —which is fought by hiding a bomb in a student cafeteria."

"There may be civilians in Jordan who have been hurt, but I don't think anybody can say rightly that Israel has attacked civilians there. If the Al Fatah camps are built near villages in Jordan, when the camps are attacked it may be that civilians are hurt, and we are sorry about that. But certainly nobody can honestly and sincerely and fairly compare that with dynamite in our Mahane Yehuda marketplace or a mine placed in a supermarket, because a supermarket is not exactly the military base of the Israeli Army."

The year before Israel won its independence, Golda said: "We would not ask for a state if we did not think we could defend ourselves."

Nasser has said that before his country takes any action that could lead to an Israeli victory: "We think once, twice, three and four times."

Golda commented: "I recommend that he think *five* times before he begins another adventure which will end in yet another defeat."

"I don't know what the Arabs want; they always take a licking. Rationally you can't explain what they are doing—they convince themselves of things that are not real, and they haven't the courage to face facts. They can either destroy Israel—and I'm positive that will not happen—or they will have to live with us. There is no other way."

"Kings and Presidents can't mobilize their armies, attack another people, lose the battle, and then say it isn't nice to take something by force."

Asked whether Israel was doomed to live without peace, Golda replied: "One assumes that until the '67 war we had peace. We never had peace, and we lived with that for twenty years."

"There cannot be quiet on one side of the border, and shelling on the other. We will either have peace on both sides, or trouble on both sides."

"If we're allowed to live in peace, we'll be the most peaceful people in the world. If we're attacked, we'll fight back every time."

"After two years of Arab terror, there has not been one execution in Israel. Instead of executing terrorists, we destroy houses which shelter them. So knocking down a house becomes a barbaric act!"

Late in 1963, Golda said: "Some months ago Nasser said that he would attack when he was convinced that the victory would be his. We take what Nasser says seriously. We must."

"There was a man in a Czarist Russian village who always knew in advance which night the horses were going to be stolen—because he was the *gonif* (thief). When Nasser warns that there's going to be a war with Israel, how does he know? He's the *gonif*."

"On the morning of June 5, 1967, my predecessor, the late Levi Eshkol, sent a message to King Hussein [of Jordan], telling him: 'If you don't come into the war, nothing will happen to you.'

"That same morning, Hussein received another message. This one was from President Nasser, who, after the Egyptian Air Force had been practically wiped out, told Hussein: 'I have destroyed seventy-five percent of the Israeli Air Force. Come in.'

"At the same time, Nasser also sent a message to his friends in Syria saying: 'Seventy-five percent of my Air Force has been destroyed. Stay out.' "

"According to the 1947 U.N. resolution, Jerusalem was supposed to be internationalized. Maybe only a Jew, or a non-Jew who knows the Bible well, understands what it means to have a Jewish state without Jerusalem. But we accepted.

"What happened to this holy city? It was shelled by the Arabs. Not one single power in the world to whom the city is holy—not one—lifted a finger to defend it from the shells. We were the only ones who did. But the Arab Legion in 1948 was stronger than we were in this area, and they occupied the Old City.

"Every single Jew who remained alive was thrown out. The only people who could not go to their holy places were the Jews. We couldn't go to the synagogues which had been there for centuries. Who worried about it? Did anybody say: 'But look, in this place there is the Mosque, there are Christian holy places, there are also Jewish holy places; how is it that Jews are not allowed to go to their holy places?' Did it give anybody sleepless nights? Are Jewish holy places less holy than Moslem holy places?"

"We say 'Peace,' and the echo comes back from the other side, 'War.' "

"We will build Israel with decency and dignity, and one day our present detractors will come knocking at our door."

"If hatred is abandoned as a principle of Arab policies, everything becomes possible again."

even when we win

"We don't want wars even when we win."

"The Israelis have no joy in killing, no joy in shooting, no joy in winning wars."

"This time we decided it must be the real thing. Nothing synthetic. No make-believe. This must be the real thing. This must be peace."

"Our generation reclaimed the land, our children fought the wars, and our grandchildren should enjoy the peace."

"If we have to have a choice between being dead and pitied, and being alive with a bad image, we'd rather be alive and have the bad image."

"I am convinced that peace will come to Israel and its neighbors because the tens of millions of Arabs need peace just as much as we do. An Arab mother who loses a son in battle weeps as bitterly as any Israeli mother."

Golda described the Israeli soldiers of the June, 1967, war as "the saddest victorious army in history."

"If we are still alive, it is because of the price we paid and the greater price we were prepared to pay. But we don't want to raise our grandchildren to prepare for another war."

"Peace will come when Nasser loves his own children more than he hates the Israelis."

"Nasser must conclude that peace is not a luxury. It's something that his children, the children of the Nile Valley, need as much as we do."

"We believe that people should not interfere in the internal affairs of other countries. Therefore, we do not plead guilty to having elected Nasser to be head of Egypt, and we have not been preoccupied with plans to replace him. This is something entirely for the Egyptian people."

"What we hold against Nasser is not only the killing of our sons but forcing them for the sake of Israel's survival to kill others."

"We owe a responsibility not only to those who are in Israel but also to those generations that are no more, to those millions who have died within our lifetime, to Jews all over the world, and to generations of Jews to come. We hate war. We do not rejoice in victories. We rejoice when a new kind of cotton is grown, and when strawberries bloom in Israel."

the only road to peace

"The only alternative to war is peace. The only road to peace is negotiation."

"You ask us what we want, and we tell you. Is it too much to expect straight talk from Nasser as well? This attempt to interpret him is fantastic. You keep saying: 'He's an Arab and therefore we mustn't expect a straightforward answer.' Can't he have the courage of a leader and speak plainly?"

"If Nasser chooses New York for negotiations, it's all right. If he wants to go to New Jersey, that's fine too. If he says Geneva, we agree. I'm even prepared to go to Cairo—how about that!—to sit down at the table."

"Arab officials will have to overcome the shock of meeting us—not on the battlefield, but at the negotiating table."

"As long as the illusion is nurtured in the hearts of Arab leaders that there might be a solution without negotiations, the solution is only obstructed."

"Are the Arab leaders prepared to live in peace? A demand has to be made of them to give a clear and simple answer. When we are asked this question, we say: 'Yes.' When the Arabs are asked this question, they have a hundred and one answers, but not the only one that can open the road to a peaceful solution."

"Since 1967 we have been, I won't say in conflict, but at any rate in friendly and even unfriendly discussions with our friends who ask: 'Why is Israel so intransigent and obstinate? Why do you insist that the Arabs must face you? Why do you insist on direct negotiations?'

"Friends, this is not intransigence. It's not obstinacy. We are intransigent and obstinate on one point only: We want to remain alive and independent. It's not a special luxury that Israel wants for itself, but the same as any other people. No more, but no less."

On taking office as Premier, Golda was asked if there were any points in dispute with the Arab states which were not negotiable from the Israeli point of view.

"Yes," she replied. "For instance, our being thrown into the sea. That is not negotiable. When the Arabs want to live in peace with the State of Israel, we will negotiate everything."

"Do the Arabs need another state? They already have fourteen. We have only one."

"One of the things we must do is convince people outside this area that our stand is right, that there is no alternative. I speak of convincing our friends because our enemies don't talk to us, so we can't do very much about that."

"As long as the Arabs won't talk to us, there's no reason to draw maps of what the Middle East should look like. We would have to discuss the maps either among ourselves—which would only lead to arguments—or with friends who had no part in the war. The only ones with whom we have to decide on boundaries are our neighbors."

QUESTION: At what point is Israel prepared to lay her cards on the table and say precisely what she is prepared to negotiate?

ANSWER: We will lay our cards on the table when we face representatives of the Arab countries. There is no sense in playing games by ourselves.

Golda insists that Israel's problem is not territorial, but rather the enemy's refusal to sit down and talk with Israeli representatives. "Suppose we want to return territory we have taken. To whom? We can't send it to Nasser by parcel post."

Was Israel prepared to retreat to the vulnerable pre-1967 borders? Replied Golda: "I'm sorry, so accommodating we are not."

"The Arabs now say: 'Israel must withdraw to the 1967 line.' That's exactly where we were when the war began.

"Then why did war break out? Why did Nasser, in May, 1967, mass his army in the Sinai Desert? The Sinai Desert was under his control. He didn't have to take it away from us. He massed his army there, put in tanks and bombers and guns and a hundred thousand men. What for? In order to get the 1967 line? He had it."

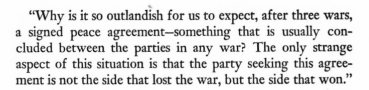

"Why is it so outlandish for us to expect, after three wars, a signed peace agreement—something that is usually concluded between the parties in any war? The only strange aspect of this situation is that the party seeking this agreement is not the side that lost the war, but the side that won."

Speaking to an audience in New York, just after Israel's victory in the Six-Day War, Golda said: "Is there anybody who can honestly bid the Israelis to go home before a real peace? Is there anyone who wants us to begin training our ten-year-olds for the next war? You say no. I am sure that every fair-minded person in the world will say no, but—forgive my impertinence—most important of all the Israelis say no."

"If Russia thinks it can prepare a peace plan acceptable to us, and has enough influence on President Nasser to get him to agree, then it has enough influence on him to say, 'For God's sake, sit down with the Israelis and make peace directly.'"

"Israel has no hawks or doves. No Israeli would refuse to yield some territory should we be offered, as a result of direct negotiations, a concrete peace treaty."

"This war is unwinnable. The Arabs won't defeat us, and we cannot conquer the Arabs. The only solution is peace. So we say: 'Come and negotiate without any preconditions. We must live together and dream dreams of what we can do together.'"

"I'm convinced that some day—I don't know when—someone—and I envy him already—will stand before the communities of the world with the message that there is peace in Israel—joy in Israel—and only joy in Israel. And we will know that everything which contributed to that day was worthwhile."

we count each one

"In Israel, we do not hide facts. Each military death is recorded. Each one who falls defending the country—his story is told, his picture is in the daily press. We count each one. And each sorrow is not only of the mother, but of all mothers, of everybody in the country. They're everybody's sons."

"The great heroes of the present generation are not only the soldiers but their wives and mothers, who are forced to say good-bye to them so often."

"We are told in the Bible not to depend on miracles, and yet we live in the land of miracles. In the June war our miracle was men and women, young and old, who fought to defend the life and independence of the country."

"The fact that the Jews have survived, the fact that we have been privileged to live in the generation in which Israel has been reborn, is due to one thing—something which many in the non-Jewish world have never understood. We are *am k'shey-oreff* (a stiff-necked people). We are a people which does not bow, a people which stands erect to face its tragedies. If we are criticized because we do not bow, because we cannot compromise on the question 'To be or not to be,' it is because we have decided that, come what may, we are, and we will be."

"On May 14, 1948, in Tel Aviv, the Jewish people condensed thirty-four centuries of their history into thirty-four minutes. On that day a nation was reborn."

When the West German government requested diplomatic relations with Israel, Golda said: "This means for every Israeli a debate between the head and the heart."

"A Jewish state that is not sensitive to discrimination would not be true to itself. We are, of course, not the only people who feel this way. Others are sensitive because of their ideology or philosophy. We have, in addition, the experience of the Jewish people."

"Every mountain, every valley in our country, tells of our belonging, of our being here. This is where we were for thousands of years, this is where we belong. The years of dispersion form one of the most tragic chapters in history. Massacres, hate, humiliation—that was our lot.

"And did the desert in Israel bloom as long as we were in exile? Did trees cover the Judean hills, were marshes drained? No—rocks, desert, malaria, trachoma—this is what the country was like before we came back."

"We are not a new people. We have not come to a new country. We are an old people that has come back to its old home."

"Somebody who came recently to Jerusalem for the first time said: 'There is light from within this city.'"

"We've seen children who didn't know how to smile, children who came to us from the camps in Germany—the few who were left after a million children went to the gas chambers. They didn't know how to sing, they didn't know what a rose was—they had never seen one grow. And now in Israel, in the north and in the south, these 'children' have made things grow—on sand and on rocks where nothing has grown for centuries."

"We have been obliged to become good soldiers, but not with joy. We are good farmers with joy. It's a wonderful thing to go down to a kibbutz deep in the Negev and remember what it was—sand and sky, maybe a well of brackish water—and to see it now green and lovely. To be good soldiers is our extreme necessity, but there is no joy in it."

"One of the first sights that shocked me, when I came to Israel in 1921, was an Arab turning over a field with a very primitive plow; pulling the plow were an ox and a woman. Now, if it means that we have destroyed this romantic picture by bringing in tractors, combines, and threshing machines, this is true: we have."

"The only thing we have ever wanted to conquer, and did to a certain extent, is the desert. It is the only joy we have in conquest, and we do something about it."

"We've sent our experts in agriculture and building to over eighty countries, and we'd be more than happy to share our knowledge with those around us. God knows—and the people in our neighboring countries know—how much they need this help. They have the same problems we have, the same lack of water, the same desert, exactly the same."

When Billy Graham asked Golda the secret of Israel's success in Africa, she said: "We go there to teach, not to preach."

"At a meeting of American Jews, a man asked: 'What about packages to Israel?' Now, maybe this seems funny to you; it is not funny to me. I am a citizen of Israel, and I absolutely refuse to be classified as someone belonging to a people whose needs can be answered by packages."

citizens of the world

"Not only as citizens of Israel, but as citizens of the world, we are vitally interested that there should be an understanding between America and the Soviet Union, but, to say it very bluntly: Not at our expense."

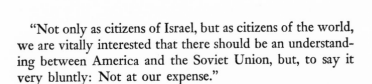

On hearing of new Soviet arms deliveries to Egypt, Golda said: "I am especially impressed when we are told that a partner to the search for peace in the area is the Soviet Union, since its contribution to peace in the Middle East has been, thus far, outstanding."

"We don't exactly regard the Soviet Union as our staunchest friend. And you can consider this an understatement."

"Our boys are killed and wounded every day by Russian bullets and shells and *Katyushas*.* In Israel, little children know what a *Katyusha* is. The Russian language has infiltrated into Hebrew."

"I don't know whether the Soviet Union wants war, but I don't think it wants peace. What would friend Kosygin do then? He can be here only as long as Nasser needs planes and tanks. If there's no destruction, he's out of the picture."

"The most realistic regime in the world," Golda said of the Soviet government. "No ideals."

* A *Katyusha* is a Soviet-built mobile rocket launcher.

On hearing reports that Soviet authorities were deporting people from Hungary in 1956, Golda told the U.N. General Assembly: "My delegation cannot refrain from speaking on this question. We have had such an intimate knowledge of boxcars and of deportations to unknown destinations that we cannot be silent."

"I have reason to envy Mr. Abba Eban as Foreign Minister for many things. But especially for one thing: He will never have to do what I had to do in 1957—to stand before the United Nations and say we will withdraw. I did it on behalf of the government, but that was not my finest hour."

"We are members of the United Nations; so are the Arab states. It seems to me that the United Nations should make the kind of situation impossible in which one member state does not recognize the existence of another."

"I am beginning to feel sorry for the Security Council, which sits there and discusses us. It might make more sense if the Knesset were to pass judgment on the Security Council."

In 1948, when Israel was asserting its independence, Golda said: "Those responsible for British policy cannot forgive us for being a nation without their approval. They cannot understand that the problem of the Jews of Europe was not created for the sole purpose of embarrassing the British government."

Charging that its sovereignty had been violated when Eichmann was kidnaped from its territory and brought to Israel, Argentina brought a complaint to the Security Council.

"Is this a problem for the Security Council?" Golda asked. "This is a body that deals with threats to the peace. Is the trial of Eichmann by the very people to whose physical annihilation he dedicated all his energy a threat to the peace, even if the manner of his apprehension violated the laws of

Argentina? Or did the threat to peace lie in Eichmann at large, Eichmann unpunished, Eichmann free to spread the poison of his twisted soul to a new generation?"

"We must do all in our power to help the illegal immigrants," Golda declared in 1940. "Britain is trying to prevent the growth and expansion of the Jewish community in Palestine, but it should remember that Jews were here two thousand years before the British came."

"De Gaulle couldn't forgive us because he was proven wrong. He prophesied two things—that this time Nasser would throw us into the sea, and that there would be a world war."

these people belonged

＊＊ ＊＊

"After the First and Second World Wars, there were millions of refugees. Somehow solutions have been found for all—Pakistanis, Indians, Sudeten Germans—all kinds. Somebody to whom these people belonged was interested in solving their problems.

"The Arab refugee problem was not solved because the governments of the Arab countries refused to solve it, because they used the misery of the Arab refugee as one of the weapons against Israel."

＊＊

"There is no Zionism except the rescue of Jews," Golda said in 1943.

"The period since we won our independence has been the first—for many, many centuries—during which the words 'Jewish refugee' are no longer heard. There is no such thing any more because the Jewish state is prepared to take every Jew, whether he has anything or not, whether he is a skilled worker or not, whether he is old or not, whether he is sick or not. It doesn't make a particle of difference."

In 1946, Golda said: "We have many grievances against the [British] government. . . . But the chief accusation that we have is that the policy of [Britain's] White Paper forced us to sit here helpless at a time when we were convinced we could have saved hundreds of thousands, and if only tens of thousands, if only one Jew!"

"I was born in Czarist Russia. I lived in the pale. I am afraid that our youngsters will look down upon the Jews in the ghetto because they did not fight. But in their very preservation of life, Jewish life, there was heroism. Our youngsters who have grown up in the atmosphere of modern Israel often say: 'How could six million people go to the gas chambers? Why didn't they fight?'

"But how do you fight under a regime of that kind? (In any case, I believe that anyone who has not been there has no right to pass judgment.) To me the very fact that people in the ghetto organized dramatic circles, music lessons, and literature classes is evidence of their heroism. What, after all, did the Germans want? Not only to kill Jews. They wanted to bring the Jew to the state where he was no longer a human being. So to me the heroism in the ghetto did not start on the day when they rose against the Germans with what arms they had, but throughout their whole life there. When rabbis went at the head of the group to the gas chambers, they went with prayer, saying *'Ani ma'ameen'* ('I believe'). They did not go with bowed heads, crying. I want our youngsters to know, appreciate, and respect that."

"The new immigrants are heroes in their way—heroes because they have remained Jews. The places where they come from, it takes a lot of heroism to remain a Jew."

seventy is not a sin

"Being seventy is not a sin. It's not a joy, either."

"I can say honestly that never in my life have I planned what position I would like to have. I planned to come to Palestine. I planned to go to a kibbutz. And I planned to be in the Labor movement. But what position I would occupy? Never."

When people ask Golda if she feels handicapped at being a woman Minister, her answer is: "I don't know—I've never tried to be a man."

On March 18, 1969, Golda gave her first press conference —for the foreign press, in Jerusalem—after becoming Premier.

QUESTION: When your appointment was first mooted, you said you'd be a stopgap. Do you expect to be a stopgap?

ANSWER: Did I say I was a stopgap?

QUESTION: You didn't, but others did.

ANSWER: They should be asked the question.

"It has been my good fate—or otherwise, I don't know— to work from an early age mainly among men, and it is to their credit, I suppose, that I always felt pretty good about it. I never expected any privileges from anybody because I was a woman, and the men with whom I worked never treated me less kindly because I was a woman. They never gave in to any argument because I was a woman, and they always had the courage to accept my idea, if they thought it was right. And if not, I accepted the majority idea although it was an idea mainly made up by men."

"The kibbutz made me an expert in growing chickens. Before that I was afraid to be in a room with even one chicken."

When Golda was Foreign Minister, she worked an eighteen-hour day. After two years, her Chief of Cabinet suggested that Golda take a vacation.

"Why?" she asked. "Do you think I'm tired?"

"No," he said, "but I am."

"So *you* take a vacation," Golda rejoined.

"I have raised two children. I can rationalize that my children are no worse than children whose mothers stayed home. They have a very close relationship with me, but if I am to be honest with myself there is a little—maybe more than a little—pang of conscience over the injustice I have done them, days or evenings I should have remained with them but couldn't."

When Golda heard a highly dramatic version of her appeal to President Kennedy for arms with which to defend Israel, she rejoined: "If I had spoken to Kennedy *so* beautifully, I would have gotten more arms."

In 1968 Golda resigned as head of the Labor Party. "I want to be able to live without a crowded calendar," she said. "I want to be able to read a book without feeling guilty, or go to a concert when I like."

Then she added: "But I do not intend to retire to a political nunnery."

Referring to Jewish assimilation in the United States: "My American friends worry about their grandchildren. My grandchildren are in the Negev in a frontier kibbutz, but I don't worry about them. They are safe."

To young volunteers who came to Israel during the Six-Day War, and were preparing to return home, Golda said: "You were ready to die with us. Why don't you want to live with us?"

Recalling the days of pogrom in Czarist Russia, Golda told one audience: "If there is any explanation necessary for the direction which my life has taken, perhaps it is the desire and the determination to save Jewish children from a similar scene and from a similar experience."

"Three or four days before the 1967 war I went down to the Negev to visit my daughter and grandchildren—just to see them, not being sure what might happen.

"I said three things to them: 'I don't see how war can be avoided. Nobody is going to help us. I'm convinced we will win.'"

"When I saw King Hussein on television in the United States I was reminded of the story of the man who had killed his father and was up for murder. He pleaded with the judge, 'Have pity on me; I'm an orphan.'"

"I want to admit that when I came to the United States at the invitation of the President, I was scared. Scared because of the responsibility that rests on my shoulders to represent Israel. It isn't simple. Israel is so big in spite of its smallness—one must be conscious of one's inability to represent it properly. But I have that—the consciousness of the inability."

From a press conference at the National Press Club in Washington:

QUESTION: Your grandson, Gideon Meir, age seven, says that you are the best gefilte fish maker in Israel. What is your recipe?

ANSWER: My grandson . . . I'm afraid he's maybe not very objective about me. I'm not very objective about him, either.

When foreign statesmen are prepared to see Israel make any sacrifice, Golda recalls a story about a stingy father and a generous mother. The mother insisted that her husband bring people home from the synagogue for Friday-night dinner, and she would begin by serving them pickled herring.

"All right," he said, "you have to feed them, but do you have to build up their appetites?"

"After fifty years of living in what is now Israel, I think in Hebrew—except in arithmetic."

"I don't want to have a bad influence on anybody, but there's no point in my giving up cigarettes now. I won't die young."

"When I came to Palestine in 1921, the heavy industry was chocolate. And when I asked, 'Why does it taste so sandy?' I was told, 'Sand is our only natural resource.'"

Golda was one of the thirty-seven signers of Israel's Declaration of Independence. "After I signed, I cried," she said. "When I studied American history as a schoolgirl and I read about those who signed the Declaration of Independence, I couldn't imagine these were real people doing something real. And there I was sitting down and signing a Declaration of Independence."

Just before Israel won its independence, Golda, dressed as an Arab woman, went to see King Abdullah. He asked her not to hurry proclamation of the state. She rejoined: "We have been waiting for two thousand years. Is that hurrying?"